Contents

Introduction

Life entails inevitable challenges. To surmount these battles, we each seek for various mechanisms. This particular eBook on Dialectical Behavior Therapy (DBT) is developed for those who are struggling with Borderline Personality Disorder (BPD), depression, anxiety, and other psychiatric disorders. It will also be a great resource for those who have loved ones beset by the same issues.

In the course of this eBook, you will understand what DBT is, its benefits, and its four core modules: mindfulness, interpersonal effectiveness, emotional regulation, and distress tolerance.

Each module is elaborately addressed in this eBook with instructive exercises and worksheets to help you (or someone around you) understand, control, describe emotions, cope with distressful situations, and much besides through DBT.

Borderline Personality Disorder (BPD) and its connection with DBT are also dilated upon.

This eBook will bestow you a beneficial and strong foundation of DBT that will serve as help if you decide to pursue this avenue.

What is Dialectical Behavior Therapy (DBT)?

Dialectical Behavior Therapy (DBT) is a therapeutic method that merges cognitive-behavioral procedures and mindfulness to impart individuals the skills to keep their emotions under control, improve relationships with people around them, and manage distressful circumstances.

Dialectical Behavior Therapy was first realized in the 1970s in Washington by Marsha Linehan, a psychologist researcher. It was developed for the treatment of women with Borderline Personality Disorder (BPD). It has since proven success and is extensively used for an array of psychological disorders, including anxiety disorders, depression, eating disorders, and addiction.

Research Facts about DBT

Research proving the advantages of DBT for various people suffering from different kinds of mental ailments is abounding. Those who have taken up on DBT, ones suffering from borderline personality disorder (BPD) in specific, have shown notable improvements; reduction in self-harm attempts and depression were but a few. Improvements in feelings of hostility, fury, hopelessness and detachment were also noted.

It has also been found that, people who have completed the DBT program designated less participation in premeditated self-harm and suicidal attempts.

Recent studies have shown that Dialectical Behavior Therapy (DBT) is an effective treatment when used on those dealing with an eating disorder or substance addiction. Throughout the treatment, there was a significant decrease in the usage of substance and an overall improvement in their functioning.

Research still continues to support DBT as an effective technique for treating individuals who are grappling with emotional dysregulation and tolerating distress.

Borderline Personality Disorder (BPD)

What is BPD?
Borderline personality disorder is a durable mental condition that leads to the development of a self-destructive behavior in order to cope from an unstable home or a childhood trauma, particularly sexual abuse.

In accordance with the celebrated Diagnostic and Statistical Manual of Mental Disorders (DSM IV TR), people with BPD are distinguished by:

- Difficulties managing anger
- Recurrent suicidal behaviors, thoughts or attempts

- Erratic temper
- Paranoia or dissociative sign
- Unsteady interpersonal relationships
- Fear of rejection and preoccupation
- Feeling worthless on a regular basis
- Impulsive behavior
- Identity crisis

Often, people suffering from borderline personality disorder go through emotions of emptiness in tandem with insomnia, depression, destructive relationships, impulsive behavior and suicidal ideation and urges.

They also have an incredible amount of fear of being deserted by family, friends or intimate partners. They are devoid of any tolerance when it comes to living on your own and are therefore in desperate need of having people around them. Reacting impulsively with fuming outburst to avoid abandonment is part of their behavior.

In personal relationships, people with BPD initially have moderate boundaries and may disclose significant personal information – they will spend plenty of time with their partner. But then their fear of rejection or abandonment prevails and they will eventually start to alienate their partner.

It is during adolescence that borderline personality disorder commonly emerges. The symptom is aggravated during early adulthood, and might possibly persist throughout life span without treatment.

It is believed that BPD develops due to a vulnerable childhood. The vulnerability can be occasioned by parental exposures or genetics. The child is incapable of learning to manage his/her emotions efficiently, let alone understanding them when brought up in a psychologically invalidating surrounding where he/she experiences an invalid or trivial emotion.

People suffering from BDP experience a lost sense of self-esteem and identity and it is probable that they will face a variety of other psychosomatic disorders as in anxiety, depression and eating disorders.

DBT and BPD

Dialectical Behavior Therapy (DBT) is the core therapy in treating Borderline Personality Disorder (BPD).

In an intense relationship, people with BPT tend to oscillate from desiring intimacy to letting their fear of rejection prevail and pushing people away.

BPD victims contend with keeping their emotions under control. They also have a great amount of difficulties in coping with negative emotions. Often, they are emotionally sensitive and may live through intense anger, bad temper or anxiety over an extended period of time. And when rapidly engulfed by these negative emotions they tend to resort to deliberate self-harm or substance abuse.

DBT targets to resolve urgent issues such as suicidal behavior.

Individuals with Borderline Personality Disorders who enroll themselves in DBT will successfully obtain the skills needed to standardize their feelings and reduce overpowering deleterious emotions. Once effectively undergoing a Dialectical Behavior Therapy program, a BPD sufferer often feels empowered to cope with a range of psychosocial issues.

Who Benefits from DBT?

Whether you are contending with problems related to impulse control, interpersonal relationships, self-injurious behavior, or emotional regulation, DTB will assist you in transfiguring your behaviors and feel like yourself again.

Dialectical Behavior Therapy (DBT) treatment targets the following problem areas:

- Depression and anxiety issues
- Emotional Dysregulation
- Interpersonal relationships
- Self-harm, such as cutting
- Suicidal thoughts, urges, and attempts
- Impulse control

- Issues related to trauma
- Self-esteem issues
- Substance abuse
- Eating disorder
- Other high-risk behaviors

Session Structure

Dialectical Behavior Therapy (DBT) entails three components: Individual, group, and phone coaching.

1. **Individual Therapy**: In this section the patient and therapist have an ongoing discussion about the incidents that occurred throughout the week. This conversation will be documented in a journal. Suicidal behaviors and intentional self-harm are the primary subjects in individual therapy. These sessions are once a week and typically last for an hour-and-a-half.

2. **Group Therapy**: clients attend a two to two-and-a-half hour weekly skills training over a twelve month period. Certain groups may conduct a biweekly session. Group dynamics and cohesion is this modules central focus. It is basically a skills training.

3. **Phone Coaching**: this module is intended to help simplify skills into the patient's everyday life. Phone coaching is concise and focuses on skills. If you are envisaging self-harmful behavior, you are urged to

participate in these sessions with your selected therapist.

Structured in four stages, DBT has specific objectives:

Stage 1: Taking control of one's behavior

Objective 1: Decrease and then eradicate self-endangerment behaviors such as suicidal thinking, suicide attempts or intended self-harm.

Objective 2: Curtail and then eliminate deeds that intrude with treatment. The main aim is to address behaviors that can bring the treatment to an early end; for example, behavior that "burns out" people who try to support and other therapy-interfering actions.

Objective 3: Reduce manners that are damaging to the quality of life, such as depression, neglect of health and hygiene, eating disorders, phobias, substance misuse and much besides. Behaviors that may ameliorate life satisfaction include: physical well being, having friends, active enrollment in work or school, having adequate housing and finances.

Objective 4: Pick up skills to help control your attention, in order to cease obsessing about the past or fretting about the future. The new skills will help increment mindfulness of the "current moment", obtain an understanding of what actually makes you feel good or bad, and tolerate emotional pain.

The four main modules that will be dilated on later in this eBook include:

- ➢ **Core mindfulness skills:** This DBT skill allows the way for you experience your senses while being fully aware and alive in the present. Mindfulness will also help you increase attentiveness.
- ➢ **Interpersonal effectiveness:** Interpersonal effectiveness skills will equip you will all that's needed for you to get what you need, enhance the relationships you have with family or friends, and deal with interpersonal conflict in an undisruptive manner.
- ➢ **Emotion regulation:** With Emotional regulation skills you will be able to better classify your emotions, curtail emotional reactivity, manage your emotional well-being, and ameliorate emotional steadiness.
- ➢ **Distress tolerance:** This DBT skill will help you better tolerate distress and improve impulse management.

The main objective of these skills is to cultivate the individual's capacity to control their thoughts, behaviors, and emotions.

Stage 2: Experiencing emotions fully

This is a stage where clients are guided to experience emotions without shutting down, avoiding life, or suffering from symptoms of Post-Traumatic Stress Disorder (PTSD). The therapist will teach the client how to go through all of these feelings without allowing the emotions to govern. This will facilitate the way for the patient to go through and analyze all the negative emotions with ease.

Stage 3: Establishing a normal life, solving everyday problems

Once the individual has learned to control his/her emotions and manage all behavior, they will be able to manage all of their ordinary problems as in their relationships, study, work, finances and much besides.

Stage 4: Stepping towards fulfillment/connection

The last stage of DBT entails helping the participant feel complete and connect with the world. A feeling of emptiness or disconnection may linger even after undergoing stages 1 to 3. For this reason, this stage involves fusing the patient's identity with the achievements of the previous three stages.

Mindfulness Module

"If you pay attention to where your mind is at, it's not in the present. It's off somewhere else. Either in the future or the past" —Jon Kabat Zinn

You might be having a snack while watching a show on T.V or reading through a rather uninspiring article, when you're mind just wonders off. Perhaps you are thinking of the day's event or tomorrow's hectic schedule, but you most certainly are not giving attention to anything you're doing presently.

How often does that happen to you? Probably, more often than you can count. The greatest portions of our lives are spent in our absence. We do one thing while thinking of something else—we never are wholly in the moment.

Now, why does that happen? Well, to phrase it nicely, "We are automatons of our emotions and thoughts. They dictate how we think, react and unfortunately how we live. We're automated to react in a certain pattern that has already been inscribed on our brain.

Mindfulness is about tipping the balance; it allows you not only to dethrone, but to regulate your emotions and thoughts. You start scraping off those inscriptions and start creating your own patterns of reaction to situations and patterns of thinking. Mindfulness bestows you the chance to become present in the world you live in, to pay attention to the details that matter.

"Mindfulness is the idea of suspending one's thoughts, not buying into them, seeing them for what they are. It's about bringing an intentional awareness to thoughts and feelings and examining deliberately and dispassionately, so as not to get carried away by them... "Not looking, or finding, or trying, or thinking, but just being. Mindfulness is about paying attention to stuff"

Mark Rice-Oxley

Mindfulness is the epicenter of DBT. It is indeed an ancient concept that has existed in a lot of religious and spiritual traditions like Buddhism, martial arts, yoga, tai chi, and Taoism. Over the last three decades it has been adapted by Western psychology to treat psychological and mental health disorders.

The purpose of this module is to have the individual take control of their attention and focus it on the present without dwelling in the past or fretting about the future. Often, people are ensnarled in the anguishing experiences of their past or harrowing prophesies of the future. Mindfulness amplifies one's awareness, which in turn helps him/her exist in the here and now. Eventually one learns to prohibit the past or future from coloring any experience.

After developing the skills to have the unclouded perspective of the present, the individual can begin to understand his/her emotions and thoughts better and learn how to control them instead of being dictated by them.

The practice of mindfulness has been proven to reduce depression, irritability and anxiety; enhance mental stamina and memory; decrease chronic stress and hypertension; mitigate the impact of cancer; reduce chronic pain; relieve the dependency on substance abuse and reinforce the immune system to ward off diseases such as flu, colds and so forth.

Mindfulness allows for a healthier and happier life. It bestows you binoculars to look within and understand yourself profoundly.

"Happiness is your nature. It is not wrong to desire it. What's wrong is seeking for it outside when it is inside"
Ramana Maharshi

Three states of mind
Mindfulness tackles three primary states of mind.

Reasonable mind: This is the state where the individual takes a reasonable approach to address issues, and engages with focused attention and planning behavior.

Examples of the reasonable mind are: preparing for an event; measuring the ingredients before cooking a meal; studying for a test; scouring the net for information.

Emotion mind: This is a state of mind when the person is so overwhelmed and highly influenced by emotions that they control his/her thoughts and behavior.His/her thoughts are completely controlled by emotions. For instance, if a person is feeling anger or fear, it keeps his/her thoughts so volatile that thinking reasonably becomes near impossible. It makes the application of planning or logic hard as gathering the individual's attention is quite difficult at this state.

This mind state is disproportionately present in people who find controlling emotions challenging like those with borderline personality disorder.

Examples of the emotion mind are: going on an unplanned excursion on an impulse; paying an exorbitant price for an item just because you like it;giving a puppy a cuddle; having a fight with somebody you don't agree with; going out for a ride for the fun of it.

Wise mind: At this stage the individual acquires the intuition and the sense of what is wrong or right.

It is more like the "aha" moment. Wise mind is the coming together of the reasonable mind and the emotion mind. They are bound together by intuition.
Intuition is a feeling of knowing what is right or wrong. You can experience intuition without an intellectualapproach.

Examples of the wise mind are: following your intuition; going for what you sense is the right choice in a dilemma.

Core Mindfulness Skills
Core mindfulness skills could be categorized into two.

I. The "what" skills which comprise: observe, describe and participate. They give answers to the question, "What do I do to practice core mindfulness skills?"

II. The "How" skills. They include non-judgmentally, one mindfully and effectively. They answer the questions," What do I do to practice core mindfulness skills?"

Observe
This is the first "what" skill. Generally it's about addressing emotions and other behavioral responses—induced by certain events—without trying to eliminate them. In other words, an individual allows him/herself to experience a moment with awareness rather than leaving a situation or trying to stop an emotion.

In mindfulness exercises the individual is encouraged to observe the emotions, sensations in the body and thoughts that manifest in situations. Without reacting or being devoured by these feelings, the person is taught to study them. Preserving from all forms of judgment, he/she studies the emotions, thoughts and sensations and notices them disappear.
The technique is purposed to have the individual control his/her attention but not the experience.

To carry out this practice one needs to develop the Teflon mind— this is a mind state in which one has the capacity to allow feelings to pass by like clouds in the sky without clinging on to them.

Observe is a significant practice for those with borderline personality disorder or a traumatic history. It lets them discern sensations that occur in the mind and body and teaches them how to control it. It helps mitigate situations where emotions become too domineering.

Observe

- Pique your curiosity about your feelings.
- Observe the feelings and thoughts that arise without intensifying or weakening them. Don't try to stop them or make them last longer.

- Notice the stream of feelings and thoughts that enter and exit your mind.

- Take stock of your sensory stimulations: sent, touch, sound, and taste.

- Let every thought and emotion flow by without allowing any of them to linger.

Describe

Proceeding to the second part of learning mindfulness, one is encouraged to describe in words the thoughts and emotions that have come into his/her awareness. The individual could depict them as such:" I am feeling hurt," or "A thought of ..... came into mind."

When the person depicts them in words and expresses internal emotions, a feeling becomes a feeling and a thought becomes just a thought. The possibility of becoming engrossed in the emotions or thoughts that arise is reduced. If the situation is an infuriating matter, the individual acknowledges it as one and simply moves on instead of obsessing over it.

The first step to adapting coping strategies is to identify feelings that arise; once you know what they are you can learn to deal with.

Describe
♦ Employ words to depict your experience.
♦ Use "fact" words, call a thought "just a thought", call a feeling "just a feeling."
♦ Avoid emotional words.

Participation

Participation is about being fully present in an activity. A person fully immerses him/herself in what he/she is doing, whether it be eating, washing dishes or mowing the lawn.

The individual is encouraged to apply the mindfulness skills to everyday life and focus on the present. The skills would allow one to exist in life with awareness and thus live in the present with more control over his/her life.

This is an essential tool to guard against distress. A person who is devoid of mindful awareness in life is more susceptible to mood disorders and various mental ailments.

Participation

- Get "lost" in an activity.

- Be completely unaware of the time while doing your activity.

- Be natural.

Non-judgmental Stance

This is the part of the practice that aims to have the person disassociate his/herself from the judgment of what their feeling; in other words, the focus is on the "what" not the perceptive of the condition.

For instance, say a person feels angry. He or she simply defines it as "I feel angry." A judgmental interpretation of this feeling would be "I should not feel angry" or "Do I have any right to feel angry?" Such an evaluation of our emotions and thoughts is an impediment to learning mindful awareness. This is why the individual is taught to view and study thoughts and emotions from a neutral perspective—from a non-judgmental stance.

This could be a challenging skill to acquire for the highly self-critical ones or those with a rather low self-esteem.

Non-judgmental Stance

- Observe but don't scrutinize: take in just the facts, leave out the 'shoulds,' the 'should nots,' the 'hows' and the 'goods.'

- Detach yourself from your opinions.

- Accept each event, each moment as they arise.

- Discern the helpful, harmful, the wholesome thoughts and emotions— but don't judge.

One Mindfully

This is an essential component of mindfulness skills which teaches the participant the ability to concentrate on the Now and on just one thing at a time. The individual's undivided attention is focused not on the past or future but the present.

What is put into perspective here is the status quo; who the individual is today, what he/she is currently doing etc.

During practices, distractions may corrupt exercises but that's alright. That's actually the main objective of mindfulness: to notice the distractions and release them without attending to them.

One Mindfully

- One thing at a time. If you're driving, just drive; if you're eating, just eat. Carry out each task with full attention and presence of mind, body and soul.

- If you find yourself multi-tasking drop the other things you're doing and stick to one activity.

- Should any disruptive thoughts or emotions arise, acknowledge them and go back to what you're doing.

Effectively

This is where the person learns to focus on what works and what the most effective approach is. The individual acts duly with the full awareness of the ultimate objective, unhindered by judgment.

Effectively

- Focus on what really works. Meet your goals by doing what is necessary in a situation – the correct thing.

- Act skillfully: meet the needs of the circumstance.

- Relinquish petty distractions. Let go of futile anger, revenge and righteousness. They not only fail to work but actually pain you.

Mindfulness Exercises and Worksheets

Various forms of exercises are applied in DBT. From meditative mindfulness to everyday mindfulness—there are quite a lot which are used in individual and group therapy.

Here is a simple technique for a short meditative practice.

- Sit down comfortably and shut your eyes.
- Concentrate on your breathing, your exhaling and inhaling.
- An abrupt thought or emotion may corrupt your focus. That's okay. Acknowledge its presence and simply return to your focus on breathing.
- Don't forget that this is not an exercise to relax you but one that's to allow you to observe your state.
- Do not stop to judge or digest these fleeting thoughts and emotions. Just carry on.

Conscious breathing is an essential component of mindfulness. It is the launching pad for the focus of sensations in the body. After the acquisition of this skill, the individual can proceed to discerning other elements like anxiety, stress, sorrow etc.

Through mindful meditation one is taught to abandon all entanglements with the past or qualms of the future and concentrate on the here and now. Mindful meditation teaches the focus of one thing at a time and allows a person to study, discern and control thoughts and emotions.

Observe Exercise

- ❖ Observe your surroundings.

- ❖ Notice what is taking place around you without instantly or reflexively reacting. Awaken your senses. Take heed of the scent of the environment. Listen to the sounds.

- ❖ Allow thoughts and sensations to liberally pass you by.

- ❖ Do not let past experiences or worries of the future interrupt your focus. Concentrate on the present.

- ❖ Address your inner thoughts and feelings as they come. Do not allow them to consume you or lure you in to pondering over them,simply observe and let them fade away.

Describing Exercise

Say you have an important interview for a job you have been pinning for. You're nervous, you don't want to ruin your chance; you might even think, "I am going to fail this interview." Describe everything you are feeling.

- What are your bodily reactions? Are you perspiring? Do you feel
Nauseated? Are your jaw muscles tense?
- What are the thoughts going through your mind? What are yourthoughts about the interview?
- Ask yourself if these thoughts are really connected to the matter in hand.

Learning to describe the situation helps you understand that thoughts and feelings are different from the actual matter.

"Thoughts are just thoughts, feelings are just feelings" Marsha Linehan says. This is not to say that thoughts and feelings are not real; they are. But they are not the situation; they don't explain or prophecy events.

Apply this practice on any activity: walking, cooking, and watching TV etc.Try writing down descriptions of your thoughts and feelings.

Mindful Eating

Examine the food you are eating (let's say it's a burger). Observe your hand bringing the food towards your mouth. Take a moment to smell the food. Notice the emotions, sensations and thoughts that are induced by the smell. Feel the texture of the bread. Now take a bite. How is the food positioned in your mouth? Start chewing and observe the experiences the taste is giving you. Swallow it. Notice the muscles that contract as you push the food down your stomach.

Try eating with your non-dominant hand which would maximize your attention as it will make the experience new and awkward.

Walking Mindfully
Walking is a great opportunity to cultivate mindfulness. Movement can empower and sharpen awareness.

Choose the place for conducting the exercise. Don't obsess over your selection; just pick a spot about 20-30 feet apart and just walk back and forth. (You don't walk towards a certain destination; this will eliminate the distraction of "getting somewhere.")

Stick to the following steps as you walk:

❖ Begin by focusing on the sensation of walking on the ground. Feel what your heels sense as they are touching the floor. Observe the stepping motion on the floor. Try taking shorter strides and lifting your knees a little higher for each step. Stepping, stepping, stepping.

❖ Now reduce your stepping pace to see the lifting of your feet and its landing on the ground. Feel you toes propel you forward as your feet lifts. Lifting, stepping—lifting, stepping.

❖ Slow down further— enough to observe the shift of pressure and the shift of weight that occur from one foot to the next. Take stock of muscular movement when the foot rises; notice how it just hangs and then how it steps on the ground. Watch the shift go from one foot to the next. Stay focused on the process of lifting, stepping, shifting—lifting, stepping, shifting.

Once mastered, this can be applicable on even your busiest days. You can practice it on your way to work, supermarket—anywhere. It anchors you to the moment, making you fully present.

Exercise for One Mindfully
In no wise is learning to be fully present, fully aware of your daily tasks, interactions with others and every moment easy. And with worries about work, family, friends and money hovering over us, the endeavor becomes all the more challenging.

Here is the DBT skill One Mindfully that will help you focus on one task at a time.

❖ Relinquish all worries and disturbances.

❖ Concentrate on the here and now.

❖ Let the stream of distracting and disturbing thoughts and emotions enter and exit your mind. Just breathe.

❖ Gather your thoughts on what you're doing now. Say you're washing tableware. Direct your attention to the senses. Listen to the sound of water streaming down the sink. Feel the warm sensation of the water.

❖ Should any thoughts emerge to corrupt your focus, acknowledge them and return to your attentive state.

❖ If judgmental thoughts enter, notice yourself judging yourself and block them.

❖ Return to focus on your present task. Put aside other worries and thoughts for another time.

Mindfulness Worksheets

Observing and Describing Thoughts

Event that prompted it:

_____

_____

____

Feelings (and their intensity): _____Mad _____Sad
_____Glad

_____Scared _____Ashamed

List thoughts:

_____

_____

_____

_____

_____

Can you identify any MUSTS?

_____

_____

_____

Can you identify any SHOULDS about yourself?

_____

Can you identify any SHOULDS about others or the situation?

_____

_____

Pick a "should" thought and change that to a non-judgmental

DESCRIBE:

_____

_____

_____

Emotion regulation Module

With individuals dealing emotion dysregulation there is an overpowering amount of emotions and mood swings that can be noted. They grapple with managing their emotions, comprehending the cause of their distress and depicting their feeling in a productive fashion. It can be very troubling for the individual when emotions are rampant. Emotion regulation disorders are the primary symptoms of borderline personality disorder.

People with BPD go through an incredible amount of struggle with regulating their emotions effectively. They often feel their emotions are capricious and that they have full control over their being. If they react aggressively by being violent or angry while in the process of undergoing strong emotions, they become overwhelmed— which can destroy their relationships or self-esteem.

So as to feel impervious to negative emotions, these individuals resort to avoidant coping behaviors such as intentional self-harm or substance abuse.

The grounds to emotional dysregulation are various:

High emotions reactivity: High emotional reactivity is when one experiences feelings and emotions in a way that's very intense and rapid. According to experts, some people are more vulnerable to this condition than others. And this overpowering effect makes people who have high emotions reactivity highly susceptible to emotion dysregulation.

History of trauma: A traumatic event in an early age can hinder the growth of emotion regulation skills.

Emotionally invalidating environment: this means, as a child, that person's emotion were not validated. An emotionally invalidating environment can instigate emotion dysregulation. For instance, if parents tell their children that crying is a sign of weakness, it's only natural for the childern to suppress negative feelings and swallow their tears. Repression of emotions from early childhood could continue to adulthood.

The skills in emotion regulation training include:

1. Understanding emotions
2. Understanding the Functions of emotions
3. Experiencing emotions
4. Reducing emotional helplessness
5. Develop positive experiences
6. Opposite - to emotion action
7. Observing the facts
8. Cope ahead
9. Problem solve

1) Understanding Emotions

There are 8 primary emotions that are wired into our brain from childhood. When these emotions arise, they can cause our body to react a certain way or have certain urges.

Here is a list of primary emotions:

- *Anger*
- *Joy*
- *Sorrow*
- *Fear*
- *Guilt*
- *shame*
- *Interest*
- *Surprise*

In DBT program, you learn there are two types of emotions

- Primary emotions (the aforementioned)
- Secondary emotions (the emotional reaction to an emotion)

For instance: feeling shame when expressing anger inappropriately, feeling angry when you have a shameful response (e.g. hurt feelings), feeling fearful during the moments you're angry (perhaps were punished for feeling anger.) There are plenty more. These are NOT part of our brains or bodies, but are instilled from our family, culture or society.

To opt for a beneficial reaction, you much first know what the primary emotion (the core of your reaction) are during the moments you experience the secondary emotion.

With the reservation of judgments, emotions are surveyed.

In DBT, clients are taught to elaborate the event that incited the emotion (prompting event), as in a friend canceling on lunch. They will learn to describe the situation in their lives. The description of this particular event may be that the friend no longer wants to hang out with them. The feeling that follows the elaboration is pain and fury. The patient is then taught to observe the changes in their body which are occasioned by the feelings. He/she will then begin to identify these changes (e.g. increasing heart rate, a clenching fist, etc.). In this scenario, the client would be taught to reflect on the explanation of the event and express their feelings nakedly.

Exercise: Observing and Describing Emotions
1. What is the prompting event? (Emotions can either be a person's thoughts or reactions to occurrences in an environment.)
2. What is your interpretation of this event? (Note: most external situations don't prompt emotions; it is the depiction of the event that occasions the emotion. And remember it's not a fact but a judgment,)

3. What is your emotion after your interpretation?

   _____ Surprise _____ Anger _____ Shame _____ Interest

_____ Fear _____ Disgust _____Sorrow
_____ Joy

Example...

Prompting Event	Interpretation	Emotion
Looking at my boyfriend having a conversation with my best friend	_They are talking about me_	_Anger_
I see my sorority sister in town after telling me she was headed back home	_She doesn't want to spend time with me_	_Sadness_
There is lightning and thunder outside	_I heard stories about people dying after being struck by lightning_	_Fear_

4. How is your body responding to these emotions? (Observe and comment on your heart rate, breath, face, stomach, chest, throat, leg, head, neck, muscles, and hands.)

Example…

Prompting Event	Interpretation	Emotion	Body response
My dad had food poisoning	*He could die*	*fear*	*Shaky hands, heart racing, sick to my stomach*

4. What are your action urges with these emotions? What would you like to do? (Emotions play a huge role in prompting behaviors. Action urges include: fighting or verbally attacking, fleeing or hiding in terror, etc.)

Example…

Prompting Event	Interpretation	Emotion	Action urge
My automobile has a flat tier	*I know that some kid in the neighborhood did it*	*Anger*	*Attack verbally*

5. What was the aftereffect? (Consequences of your actions: physical functioning, behavior, thoughts, memories, and secondary emotions.)

Remember: you have the choice to change the way you interpret events and keep what you say or do under control, for it really is not necessary to act on your urges. At this moment, you will have the ability to use your physical experiences to distinguish and title you emotions.

2) Functions of Emotions

DBT addresses a triad of emotional functions:

Communication (for influential and communicative purposes emotions are used) Motivation and organization (for the purpose of motivating and organizing patients, emotions are employed)

Self-Validation (for the purposes of self-assertion emotions are employed)

a) Communication

We communicate our emotions employing nonverbal and verbal methods. We might use body and posture language or facial expressions. According to the teachings of DBT, nonverbal and verbal communications must coincide for others to understand the feelings of another person. The absence of congruent communications may result in the misunderstanding of a person with borderline personality disorder or any dysregulation problems. They tend to conceal their emotions till they reach a very intense situation.

Exercise

- Can you give an account of an event where your expression of emotion was misread?

- Can you also recall a point in your life when you may have misunderstood the true emotions of another person?

- Give examples of how the emotions of others have influenced you; and how your emotions have influenced others.

b) Motivation & Organization

Emotions are prompts that not only give us the cue to act but also assist us to surmount environmental hurdles. For example, when we witness a sense of danger, we might be tempted to act following the prompt given by our emotions. We might enter a stance of safety induced by the fear we feel. This is at times an involuntary act where little thought is put into the equation.

If, for instance, you come across a child amidst a thoroughfare where a car is speeding towards him, you might instantly be devoured by the feeling of fear. This emotion may prompt you to rush to save the kid without giving it a minutes thought. You will not be able to think of the kinds of danger that lies ahead; you will just take the action.

Another case is the anxiety that completely overwhelms us when in preparation for an imminent exam. This feeling may induce certain actions of ours. Through it is an uncomfortable feeling; this anxiety is the key to stimulate you to prepare for the exam in advance.

Exercise…

- Can you remember a moment in which you were stimulated by an emotion to act prior to thinking?

- Try to recall a point in which you circumvented an obstacle because of the help you received from your emotions (at school, a social event or home).

- During the course of this week, try to discern moments in which you are prompted to act because of your emotions.

c) Self-Validation

Emotions serve as a self-validation agent as they inform us about a situation or event. Although these emotions are always legitimate, they can, nonetheless, be invalid.

Most people struggling with borderline personality disorder are brought up in a very harsh home that is rather emotionally invalidating. They are therefore very doubtful of their emotions. At times, the emotions we feel under certain conditions may be unconscious; but at hindsight, these emotions often turn out to be valid.

For example: Say you receive an invitation to a party. But you have a certain level of reservation about the party. You have this queasy feeling of something going wrong. And once you reach the party you have this colossal fight with a friend you left with; the fight is so serious that you end up leaving the party all together—that means your queasy feeling concerning the party was valid after all.

3) Experiencing Emotions

In DBT sessions, patients are encouraged to embrace negative emotions without being overpowered by them. They are taught to depict and understand them. Coupled with the skills of mindfulness, participants learn to go through negative feelings; then, without allowing these emotions to drive them to detrimental actions, individuals are taught to release them. Getting a distance from emotions and observing them is also what DBT teaches its clients. The separation from emotions helps individuals comprehend them and view them more clearly.

4) Reduce emotion vulnerability

Biological factors are targeted to help patients reduce their level of vulnerability when encountering negative emotions. Linehan employs these phrases as a way of remembering these skills:

"PLEASE MASTER"

Treat PhysicaL illness

Balance Eating

Avoid mood-Altering drugs

Balance Seep

Get Exercise

Build MASTERY

A variety of biological factors may impact our emotions and mood. If we are feeling sick, hungry, tired, physically inactive or under the influence of drugs, we are prone to be susceptible to negative emotions or to the negative approach of many situations. Sustaining a positive state of mind and a healthy lifestyle, can help you get a lofty insight and control over your emotions and the experiences you encounter.

P&L: Treat Physical illness

Do you have a physical ailment that needs to be tended to? Do you have prescribed medication or treatment that you're not taking or doing? Invest some time to ruminate on this and try to tend to your well-being to the best of your abilities.

E: Balance Eating

How well do you eat? What types of food to you eat? Do you consume too little or too much? (Consuming too little means your body is lacking the nourishment it needs. Also, if you eat too little over a period of time, your body goes into hunger mode and burns the food more slowly, so it could protect itself from starving).

Eat a balanced diet; over eating or under eating will not do. Be sure to maintain a balance in your blood sugar.

A: Avoid mood-altering drugs

Alcohol and drugs can minimize endurance to some negative emotions. Some people find that alcohol makes them feel more depressed and sometimes frightened. Try noticing how alcohol and drugs makes you feel if you use them. If they pose as an issue in your life, is it possible for you to get help?

S: Balance Sleep

Certain people are good with 5-6 hours of sleep; others need 9-10 hours. But how much sleep makes you feel good?

Sleep is an integral part of life and you need to make a schedule in order to obtain the sleep you need. Lack of sleep could make a person irritable, short-tempered, disgruntled and much more.

Do you have troubles sleeping? You will find tips for a good night sleep at the end of this segment.

E: Get Exercise

Do you exercise regularly? If not, you could start out at a low pace, taking it step by step.

There is a legion of benefits in exercising. Exercise is good for our hearts, lungs, muscles and bones. Furthermore it stimulates chemicals in our brain called endorphin which are natural antidepressants.

MASTER: Build MASTERY

Do things that give you a sense of control, competence and confidence every day. Do something that you are good at—without holding back.

Can you learn a new skill? What kind of things gives you a sense of mastery? Challenge yourself, even if it is just a little.

Tips for Good Sleep

1. Only sleep for the amount time needed to invigorate you the next day. The time limit you set for your sleep only allows for deeper rest; too much time in bed could result in a fragmented and shallow sleep.

2. Pick the same time to wake up every day. This is for all the seven days of the week.

3. Minimize the consumption of all caffeine products. Beverages and foods which contain caffeine (coffee, tea, chocolate and cola) can produce difficulties falling asleep. Even an early cup of coffee in the early hours of the day can tamper with nighttime sleep.

4. Steer clear from alcohol, in the evenings especially.

5. Rid your bedroom of any noise or light.

6. Don't go to bed hungry. A bed time snack which comprises carbohydrates can facilitate sleep, but try avoiding greasy or heavy foods.

7. Exercise frequently— it facilitates for deep sleep.

8. Don't smoke when you're finding it difficult to sleep, for smoking can corrupt your sleep.

9. Try not forcing your sleep. This will only exacerbate your condition. Instead read a book in the next room and avoid engaging in a stimulating activity; when you're feeling sleepy return to your bed.

10. Don't pay attention to the clock. Toss it somewhere out of your sight, as it will only make you worried and disgruntled.

11. Avoid naps during the day so you can fall asleep well at night.

12. Clear your mind when you go to bed. Avoid going to bed with all your worries; choose another time during the day for it. Stress and anger may interfere with your sleep.

5) Build Positive Experiences
Participants of DBT are exhorted to make positive changes in their lives so that pleasant experiences occur more often. There are two ways to build positive emotional experiences:

Short Term: take part in delightful activities that you can find **NOW**.

This could be swimming, walking in the park, watching TV shows, etc. Create a list of delightful activities you can engage in daily. At the very least, MINDFULLY conduct one or two of these leisure interests. On your diary card note down the activities you have done.

Long Term: To become rewarded by the blessing of frequent positive experiences, make fundamental changes. As Marsha Linehan says it—build a "life worth living."

- Work towards your goals. Everyone's goals vary. For some people, it could be going to school, moving into a new apartment, moving to the city, etc.

    What do you want? Make a list of small steps that would help you reach your ultimate objective. Start with making the first step.
- Attend to relationships. Repair old relationships that you really care about.
- Seek out new friends.
- Strive to enforce current relationships. This might include partners, coworkers, spouses, siblings, friends, children, etc.
- Avoid **AVOIDING.** Avoid giving up.

Be Mindful of Positive Experiences

- → **FOCUS** on happenings that are (**even those one might deem petty).**
- → While you partake mindfully in a joyful experience, refocus your mind when it wanders to past regrets, current distractions, future doubts and other feelings.
- → Make a record of matters that corrupt your experience of full enjoyment. Do not falter to **TURN** the **MIND** when such happenings occur.

Be Unmindful of Worries

Distract yourself from:

Contemplating on when the delightful occurrence **WILL END**.

Contemplating on whether you are worthy or unworthy of the delight.

Contemplating on how many **EXPECTATIONS** you are expected to fulfill.

Emotion Regulation Handout

Joyful Events List

- Meditating
- Indulging in a warm bath .
- Making plans for the future.
- Completing something.

- Playing a game.
- Reminiscing good times.
- Relaxing.
- Watching TV.
- Reading a book.
- Lying /Sitting in the sun.
- Laughing out loud.
- Painting.
- Drawing.
- Singing.
- Playing an instrument.
- Remembering beautiful scenery.
- Looking outside.
- Watching the birds.
- Watching a movie.
- Gardening.
- Meeting a friend.
- Repairing something.
- Exercising.
- Indulging in a restful evening.
- Gardening.
- Arranging flowers.
- Partying.
- Praying.
- Cooking.
- Creating a present for someone from scratch.
- Getting your picture taken by a professional.
- Daydreaming.
- Listening to music.
- Taking a walk.
- Watching sports.
- Playing sports.
- Writing a diary.
- Dancing.
- Cleaning.
- Discussing books.
- Having lunch with a friend.
- Playing cards.
- Having a political discussion.
- Looking at/showing photos.
- Shooting Pool.
- Learning to play a new card game.

- Learning to play a new game.
- Reflecting on how I've improved.

- Helping a friend cope.

6) Opposite – to emotion action

Despite the emotional urge that individuals have when going through intense emotions, they are taught to act against those impulses. For instance, if a person is very enraged or anxious, he/she could act in opposition to the emotions felt and extend his/her legs and arms away from the body. This allows the individual to have control over the intense emotions felt and bestows him/her the power to change emotion states by reacting differently.

Employ the methods below to change your emotions by reacting oppositely to the present emotion.

FEAR

→ Act of your fears by doing what you are most afraid of OVER and OVER again.

→ APPROACH places, events, people, tasks and activities you are fearful of.

→ Indulge in activities that give you a sense of MASTERY and control.

→ Prepare a list of steps you can take when you're overwhelmed.

→ Do the FIRST THING you have on that listing.

GUILT OR SHAME

When shame or guilt merits JUSTIFICATION (the emotion coincides with your wise mind values)

- **FIX** the transgression.
  - a) APOLOGIZE. Say you're sorry (it will immensely help).
  - b) Care for the individual you have hurt; do something nice for him/her.
- **COMMIT** not to make the same mistake in the future.
- **ACCEPT** the outcome gracefully.
- Then **ABANDON ALL REMANANT EMOTIONS.**

When shame or guilt doesn't merit JUSTIFICATION (emotion does not coincide with your wise mind values)

SADDNESS OR DEPRESSION

- Become ACTIVE.
- Indulge in an activity the leaves you feeling ACCOMPLISHED and SELF-CONFIDENT.

ANGER

- Softly AVOID any confrontations with someone you are at odds with; instead of attacking.

(Also, erase all thoughts of the person.)

- Go for doing something NICE for someone instead of attacking them or being unkind.
- Instead of blaming, visualize EMPATHY and

7) Check the facts

Individuals taking DBT are taught the ability to discern whether their comprehension of an event is fact or fiction. If all the facts of a situation are distinguished from the illusions, the individual can avoid the extended anxiety that comes from the misconception of events. The application of different assumptions and thoughts that coincide with the facts can help the struggling individual react differently and healthily to experiences.

8) Cope ahead

DBT participants prepare in advance for emotionally charged occurrences to cope better. Emotional situations may be coped more skillfully if they prepare or rehearse beforehand. This is beneficial to the client who is waiting for a result of an event where only a few possibilities are known. The client will therefore be able to rehearse and discover coping mechanisms he/she can employ when put in a challenging situation.

9) Problem Solve

The rate of recurrence and strength of negative emotions will recede when the individual acquires the skill to consistently resolve his/her emotional issues. The individual learns effective avenues to resolve emotional problems, once he/she is able to distinguish the necessary facts of an occurrence.

In DBT, emotion modulation skills give the individuals the ability to recognize and comprehend their emotions. It also provides them with the better understanding of challenging situations and thereby permits them to employ effective coping strategies.

Interpersonal Effectiveness Module

Without having a sound interpersonal skill, building or maintaining an upright relationship in social circles, personal affairs, or the workroom is quite close to impossible. And there is that conflict, that moment of furry or disappointment, that goes hand in hand with relationships. And yes, some really do have the ability of effectively maintaining their interpersonal affairs, which is more or less the reason why they often succeed in life. But not everyone has the aptitude of handling conflict or confrontation in a way that won't damage one's emotions or the relationship itself. Not everyone can assertively set out boundaries and say NO.

Having a strong interpersonal skill is crucial and extremely beneficial for everyone. It's the way through which we can enhance our personal relationships, social affairs, and professional life. The primary benefactors of this module are ones who have suffered from Borderline Personality Disorder (BPD).

In DBT participants are taught to develop strong and healthy interpersonal effectiveness skills. With these skills participants will have the competency to:

Deal with relationships: Through the teachings of DBT's Interpersonal effectiveness skills training you will learn how to say no to things that merit rejection; terminate detrimental relationships; ask for help; address an issue promptly and deal with conflicts appropriately.

Balance priorities: Advanced interpersonal skills allow participants to distinguish their priorities in life and tend to them accordingly.

Create a balance between the shoulds and Wants: The things you should do and the things you want to do might not always relate. It's more like being stuck in a situation where you are given the choice of either going out and having fun with friends or staying indoors and studying for an exam due next week, or working on a business proposal. DPT's interpersonal effectiveness skill training helps you create the balance between work and recreation.

Build mastery and self-respect: The best part about independence is the confidence it instills in you when socializing with others. A lot of people suffer from low self-esteem because they feel helpless and dependent. Interpersonal skills provide you with all that's needed to make you feel in control of your own life, your decisions and emotions. Upon the conclusion of this module you will have a deeper comprehension and a greater respect for yourself.

Interpersonal effectiveness skill training sets before you three main objectives.

Getting what you want (Objective effectiveness)

Objective effectiveness is a guide that teaches you ways to employ your interpersonal skills to get hold of the things you want from other people. Whether its attention, respect, a pen, or a book, you will be able to acquire it if you study and practice the guidelines provided in this section. But it might not work all the time and it surly doesn't have the hypnotic power that can literally get you whatever you want, but it does work if practiced appropriately.

 In addition, the techniques used in Objective effectiveness training will not only give rise to your self-esteem but also grant you the skill of resolving interpersonal conflicts.

Objective effectiveness training is best employed and remembered when practicing with the use of the acronym **DEARMAN.**

D—*Describe:* Give out a full and honest description of the current situation. Describe all there is in your surroundings— the facts— and not what you feel about it.

E—*Express:* Not many people have the profound ability of reading minds. So you have to express and clarify what you feel about the situation. Do not swallow your opinions; communicate them with another person.

A— *Assert:* You know what you want and need out of a situation, so don't hesitate to assert it. Straightforwardly, ask for the things you want or clearly say 'No'.

R— *Reinforce:* A simple gesture as that of 'Thank you' can go a long way. So if you are to acquire what you desire, reinforce or guarantee a constructive result for that other person. Let them know that you are neither an ingrate nor a tyrant.

M— *Mindful:*This is no time for distraction. Keep your focus on the objective and no matter what conspicuous pop-ups might arise in that situation, maintain that focus. One way of sustaining your stand in such circumstances is by persistently voicing your request. You might sound like a broken record but if it gets the job done then who cares.

And if you are in a situation where that other person declares threats and attacks then simply ignore. Do not react; if you do, then, you have most certainly lost.

A— *Appear confident:* Whether you have a full-fledged confidence or not really doesn't matter; all that's needed and all that matters is you assuming the traits of someone with an impregnable confidence. Appear competent enough to handle anything; use the appropriate body language and eye contact, speak with composure and in a self-assured tone of voice.

N— *Negotiate:* If the circumstance doesn't allow the way for your request to be met promptly, then seek out alternate solutions and try to come to a comfortable bargain.

DEAR MAN Worksheet

1. **<u>Depict</u>** the status quo. Stick to the facts.

   _____

   _____

   _____

   _____

   _____

2. **<u>Express</u>**what you feel about the situation. Understand that others can't read your mind; they can't see the struggle you face to ask for what you want
   directly._____

   _____

   _____

3. **Assert** yourself by asking for what you want or saying 'no' clearly. Understand that others can't read your mind; they can't see the struggle you face to ask for what you want directly.

_____

_____

_____

_____

4. **Reinforce** the reward to the person ahead of time.

_____

_____

_____

_____

5. **Mindfully** keep your focus on your objectives. Maintain your position. Don't be distracted.

_____

_____

_____

_____

6. **Appear Confidant** Use a confidant voice tone and physical manner; make good eye contact. No

stammering, whispering, staring at the floor, retreating, saying "I'm not sure," etc.

_____

_____

_____

_____

_____

7. **<u>Negotiate</u>**, ask yourself what you're willing to settle for or relinquish in order to gain what you want from the situation?

_____

_____

_____

_____

_____

Relationship Effectiveness (Keeping the Relationship)

For so many people relationships are difficult to build. And the inevitable occurrence of conflict and confrontation in relationships makes the journey all the more scarier, especially for those who have undergone BPD.

People with BPD are once who suffer the most from interpersonal instability. On so many occasions, people dealing with this disorder have chosen to give up on their social interaction and stay secluded.

But even the faintest interaction with others can allow the formation of a good relationship, so the challenge is basically in what comes next— keeping or improving the relationship.

It is one thing, to build an upright relationship with someone, be it a coworker, a friend, a family member, or a loved one, but it's another thing to maintain its life and vigor.

We are only human and so we are highly susceptible to anger, frustration and exhaustion due to the many unpleasant circumstances in life. And when we undergo such emotional changes, we tend to take it out on our loved ones and severely mar our relationship with them.

And then there are those moments of conflict, where ideas clash, harsh words echo and all comes to ruin.

Relationship Effectiveness is the segment that's to help you improve your relationship with others through communication. It is structured to educate you on how to make other people want to meet the terms of your demand; how to reject a request without having to make that person feel terrible; and how to balance short-term goals for the sake of the relationship's wellbeing.

Relationship effectiveness can be taught by the use of the acronym **GIVE.**

G – *Gentle:* Under any circumstance, avoid hostility. When you attack, threaten, or pass off negative statements for short-term gains, you will leave an indelible mark on that person, and that will greatly affect your relationship in the long term. So be gentle in your response and reaction, and regardless of how much you're tempted maintain that gentility.

I – *Interested:* When someone is speaking to you about a matter that is very significance to them, show interest in what they are discussing , even if you have to act. Be patient and listen attentively. Ask questions every now and then to assure them that you are paying attention. Unless circumstances force it upon you, do not interrupt them, maintain genuine eye contact, be sensitive to their viewpoints. And whatever you do, never disrupt the conversation by using your cellular phone.

V – *Validate:* When in a conversation the other person speaks of their true emotions and thoughts about the matter at hand, validate it for them without judgment. Acknowledge the fact that you understand what they're going through and let them know that their thoughts, feelings, beliefs and experiences are logical and understandable. Try and figure out exactly what their problem is and seek out a solution, if any. Remember that you are there to help, not judge.

This skill can either be applied in times of conflict or peace. Validation doesn't only work as an emollient factor during intense moments but it also has the power of giving strength and vigor to the relationship.

E — *Easy Manner:* Nothing good ever comes out of a person when they feel as though they are under attack. So use easy manner when having a discussion of a critical matter. Smile a little, be light hearted and at ease with yourself, so as to make that person feel comfortable and accommodating. And if you can, giving the conversation a bit of a zing by adding a light humor won't heart.

Relationship Effectiveness Exercise

To be successful in obtaining the skills of relationship effectiveness, you must first relax and answer the following questions.

1. How important is this relationship for me?

2. After this interaction, what kind of impression would I like this person to have of me?

3. I want to keep (improve) this relationship; what must I do to meet this goal?

Self-respect Effectiveness

If you don't respect yourself, how in the world could you expect others to respect you? Everything begins and ends with you; your decisions, actions and reactions to the endless stream of things in life are what make out the gloom and glare of your life.

In this section you will be able to learn how you can heighten the positive feelings you have towards yourself and respect your own believes and values.

Self-esteem or Self-respect effectiveness skills can be memorized and practiced using the acronym **FAST.**

F – *Fair:* There is nothing decent about taking advantage of other people. It is morally degrading and it will deter your achievements in obtaining your self-respect. So aim to get hold of the things you want from other people by being fair to yourself and others.

A – *No Apologies:* We are human beings and so making mistakes is only part of our nature. But for some reason, it is easier for us to climb a mountain than admit our errors and issue an apology. It takes a great deal of courage and morality to apologize. So by declaring your heartfelt apology you would only be gaining respect from others and from yourself.

Apologies, however, have to be used sparingly and only when glaring errors are present. You should not say 'I'm sorry' for asking questions, or for the things you want; you should not apologize for being alive, sad, happy, frustrated, or exhausted. You have the right to voice an opinion and disagree with other viewpoints, so why apologize?

S – *Adhere to Values:* The principles you abide by in life, the things you value most, and your beliefs are what you must never abandon, despite the situation you're in the middle of. Do not forsake the things you stand for in order to acquire something you desire from others.

T – *Truthful:* Lies are much like the slithering snake that prowls in the veil of shadows until time permits and it attacks with its venomous fangs. No lie has ever stayed dormant forever; on that one misfortunate day it will be uncovered and when it does it will cause a great deal of damage to your relationship. So be honest, truthful about everything. Do not exaggerate or make excuses, dash it out on the plate and let it take its course.

Self-respect Effectiveness Exercise

Answer the following questions then practice the **FAST** skill.

1. When this interaction is over, how would I like to feel about myself?

2. To feel that way about myself, what will I have to do? What will work?

DEARMAN, **GIVE**, and **FAST** are skills that can be used separately or in conjunction. They all have a role to play in helping you balance your priorities, take better care of your relationship with others, and achieve self-respect.

Before using all these skills together at once though, you must first consider your objectives and priorities;

- Do you want to get something out of someone, say a friend, a colleague, a family member or a loved one?
- Do you want to keep or improve a relationship?
- Do you want to have self-respect?

Use the following sheet to have a better grasp of your goal and the situation. This will enhance your ability to know where and when to use your interpersonal effectiveness skills.

1. **What are the problems I have with this situation?**

   _____

   _____

   _____

   _____

   _____

   Is there an infringement on your wishes or rights? Is it your desire to have someone give you or do something for you? Are you feeling pressured and have reached a point of wanting to say no? Do you want to get your point of view or opinion taken seriously? Is there a conflict, a discord you would like to resolve?

2. **What results do I wish to obtain in this interaction?**

   Your Objective:

   _____

   _____

_____

_____

_____

3. After this interaction, what is the impression I would like to leave on this person?

Your
Relationship:_____ _____

_____

_____

_____

_____

4. After this interaction, how do I want to feel about myself?

Your self-esteem:

_____

_____

_____

_____

_____

5. What are my priorities in this situation?
(Rate your priorities as 1 (most significant), 2 (second significant), and 3 (least significant).

_____ Your Objective, _____ Your Relationship, _____ Your Self-esteem.

Features that hinder progress

Learning all there is to know about interpersonal effectiveness is one thing, but it's not enough to fulfill us; the skills need to be practiced frequently. But during the times of practice, there are certain challenges you will most likely face. Challenges that are quite feeble, but can certainly hinder your progress if you don't address them promptly.

Emotions: Anger, fear, guilt, sadness, and anxiety are all part of what makes us human. But when they go beyond the limit, they can take control of the moment or situation, cloud your judgment, and tamper with your interpersonal abilities. You have to keep your composure and learn how to control your strong emotions. The Emotional regulation skills offered in DBT can be of great help in such circumstances.

Ineffectiveness: If you have no clue about how to conduct yourself when in pursuit of something you desire; if you are not aware of how to act or speak when having a serious conversation with someone, then how could your interpersonal abilities grow?

In this particular challenge though, you happen to be very lucky as all that's expected of you to overcome this trial is PRACTICE, PRACTICE, PRACTICE.

Indecisiveness: A lot of people find difficulties in deciding on what they want to have or do. But this is some trait you can't afford to have, as it will make you feel doubtful about your priorities and interfere with your progress.

If your indecisiveness is disrupting your interpersonal achievements, then Problem-Solving skills training can help resolve this issue.

Environment: Our environment can become quite a nuisance at times. There will always be noise, distraction, interruption, and people who are incredibly rude around us. It can take a toll on your interpersonal effectiveness, but you can't let it go too far.

There is no practice, no lesson available for us to control our environment, so all we can do is accept it as it is.

Distress Tolerance Module

There are people who can overcome a crisis remarkably and there are those who are so overwhelmed by their emotions that they become debilitated.

Those unable to withstand the crisis resort to self-defeating escapes from the pain like substance abuse and self-harming behavior. This is often the case with people that have borderline personality disorder.

The distress tolerance module in dialectical behavior therapy teaches people to control radical emotional suffering induced by crisis. By building their resiliency and showing them various avenues to deal with difficult situations; it helps them adapt an effective coping strategy when dealing with distressing situations. Distress tolerance skills training equips an individual with the mechanics of tolerating emotional anguish and have him/her avoid self-destructive paths.

Distress tolerance skills give the participant short-term strategies to deal with harrowing situations. There are two kinds of methods:

Acceptance: This is a non-judgmental acceptance of the situation and oneself. This strategy accepts emotional suffering as an inseparable element of life and believes that failing to accept this actuality brings about further suffering. Breathing and awareness exercises are methods used to teach acceptance.

Crisis: These strategies are aimed at finding new ways to manage and survive without turning to self-defeating avenues. In DBT, participants are taught four crisis survival skills: contemplating the pros and cons, improving the moment, self-soothing and distraction.

Distraction
The techniques of distraction can easily be memorized through the acronym **ACCEPTS**.

A- *Activities*: You can easily distract yourself by indulging in pleasing activities like gardening, playing sports and walking. Jotting down a few of your favorite things to do can serve you during crises.

C- *Contributing:* This is about drawing your mind away from yourself. You can enroll yourself in voluntary work or do something nice for a family or friend. It will have you think of the person or the charity work and not yourself.

C- *Comparison:* This is a strategy in which you start comparing yourself with others who are striving to cope the same way. You can also compare the level of progress you've made since you first started. You could do this by watching movies or reading books about tragedies. This will give you a clear viewpoint of the distressing situation and help you see that there is worse out there.

E- *Emotion:* Here you are encouraged to work contrarily to your emotions. For instance, if you feel depressed and you just want to lie in bed all day, you are urged to go out for a walk or engage in a physically elevating activity. This is "opposite-to emotion action"; it has been discussed earlier.

P- *Pushing away:* This is about postponing the thought of a distressing situation. Imagery and practical exercises are implemented. For example, you can put moments of turmoil in a box and leave them there until you feel emotionally fitted to address them.

T- *Thoughts:* You are taught to distract yourself from negative or distressing thoughts. Reading, watching movies, writing a diary, counting from one to ten are some of the methods employed for this strategy.

S- *Sensations:* Through the use of techniques like taking a cold shower, holding ice in the hands, listening to loud music and flicking a rubber wrist band, you are taught to awaken the senses which will briefly distract you from emotional chaos, opening the door for the other distraction techniques discussed earlier.

Self-Soothing

It's quite impossible for those who love and care about you to always be around when you need them in your moments of distress or agitation. You need to adopt a survival skill that can help you overcome such challenging moments in life.

In DBT participants are taught self-soothing skills, which is the skill to nurture, comfort, and be kind to oneself. It is a fairly simple skill to adopt but for those who have suffered from Borderline Personality Disorder, it entails certain challenges.

People suffering from BPD tend to seek out validation and comfort from other people and so this independent way of curing their own ills often has a flustering effect on them.

Self-soothing skills in DBT are taught by using the five senses: **Touch, Hearing, Taste, Smell and Vision.**

Vision

There are so many beautiful, captivating things around us that we can use as a distraction during tough moments. Pay further attention to those little things; be it a wall, a colorful tile, a tree, birds, moving vehicles, flowers; and study their features as much as you possibly can. This visual distraction will give you the break needed to recollect your thoughts.

Hearing

By paying attention to the sounds around us, we can easily calm our nerves down and evade the overwhelming emotions that distressful moments ensue.

So if classical music, hip-pop, rock, or rap has that tendency of calming you down then download it on your phone or iPod and listen to them at such stressful moments. And if the situation doesn't permit you to listen to music, then listen to the sounds outside; pick one sound that captivates your interest and focus on it. Or you can just attentively listen to your own breathing.

Smell

Nothing can trigger a memory as effectively as that of odor. Your mother's perfume or your father's cologne, for instance, is unforgettable. And by focusing on those memories that the odors bring about, you can sooth yourself effectively. So go out shopping for a perfume, lotion, or deodorant that can take you back to the Eden of your childhood.

Or you can mindfully smell whatever kind of odor is around you. If, for instance, you are taking a shower or bath, take a moment to smell the soap or shampoo. Or when you are dinning, embrace and savor the essence of your meal.

Taste

Things that have a pleasant taste have a soothing effect. Have a small bit of a chocolate bar or mint and try to stimulate your taste buds. Savor it in your mouth first then focus on how your body reacts to the taste.

This is an effective method necessary to distract yourself when you're in some distressful situation. It can, however, be a challenge to those struggling with eating disorders or those who have an emotional attachment to food. So it's highly suggested you use a small chocolate bar, a peppermint, or a gum for this practice.

Touch

Some people find their utopia in messages and others in bubble baths, a clean sheet, or silk. So what is yours? Explore and identify the kind of touch that has a calming effect on you then treat yourself with it.

Improving the Moment

When overwhelmed by strong emotions, it's quite impossible to keep anything under control, let alone a crisis. But by staying mindful and improving the moment you would be able to tolerate the inundation of negative emotions during distressful moments.

This skill can effectively be put to practice and remembered by the acronym **IMPROVE**.

I – *Imagery:* Positive imagination is a very powerful tool that can help you keep strong emotions under control.

Picture yourself in a distressful situation; alone and deserted on an island or losing a job; then imagine the positive aspect of the scenario, which is you overcoming the crisis. This technique will take you to a safe and relaxing state of mind.

M – *Meaning:* To every downside there is an upside. Painful and stressful experiences always have a thing or two to teach us; we just have to look deeper into them. And by giving your situation a certain amount of value and meaning, you can improve the moment and overcome your throb-inducing emotions.

P – *Prayer:* You don't have to be a devout disciple of some religion to use this technique, all you have to do is believe in a higher being, be it God, the Buddha, or your own Wise Mind, to whom your prayers are directed.

There are two kinds of prayers in DBT; one is where you ask 'Why me?' In this prayer you ask the numinous entity if there is a reason, a purpose behind the pain you're experiencing in life.

And the second is where you ask for the bestowal of strength and relief.

R – *Relaxation:* To improve the moment relaxation techniques can be employed. In this practice, methods such as deep breathing, listening to music, taking a bath or progressive muscle relaxation can be employed for relaxation.

O – *One thing in a moment:* This is a technique that has much semblance to that of the teaching in Core-Mindfulness skills, which were previously discussed. By focusing on just one thing at a time, you'll be able to give yourself enough leeway to calm down and deal with crisis accordingly.

V – *Vacation:* Vacationin DBT doesn't quite necessarily mean 'going off to a holiday'. It is a metaphorical expression that basically means 'Give yourself a Break'. Grant yourself an entire day off and engage in an activity that entertains you best; read a book, go spend some quality time with your friends or relatives, treat yourself to a spa or your favorite food or drink. These activities will allow for a break from the crisis.

E – *Encourage:* When you are amidst some stressful situation, have a positive conversation with yourself. Acknowledge your efforts and encourage yourself by repeatedly saying things such as 'I can do this', 'I am doing the best I can', 'this will not go on forever', 'I will be okay'.

Remember that for any of these skills to work effectively, you need to practice.

Pros and Cons

This is a part of the distress tolerance module where the individual is asked to jot down a list of the disadvantages and advantages of tolerating and the same list for not tolerating distressful situations. He/she is asked to evaluate the consequences of potential choices. This exercise aims at having the individual focus on the long-term goals and benefits of overcoming a crisis.

Let's assume that you just got informed that your dance class was cancelled. Tolerating the distressful situation would be you accepting that you are upset, but able to understand that you'll attend the class next time. Failing to control the anguish would be you lashing out at the tutor and assuming a vituperative stance.

The consequence of your first action would be a brief moment of anguish; however, you would be able to go to your next dance class. The consequence of your latter action would be a feeling of shame after such an unreasonable reaction and a potential expulsion from your class.

Eventually, you learn that tolerating distress instead of acting on impulsion is a better option in the long run.

Radical acceptance

Radical acceptance is about accepting the situation and ceasing to fight, accepting the situation as it is rather than how you want it to be.

Radical acceptance believes that moving on is only possible when one acknowledges the fact that the past is unchangeable.

Your mind will work effortlessly to prohibit you from seeing a situation you are in as it is rather than what you want it to be. Your mind will fall back into old patterns giving you other interpretations, thoughts and ideas of the situation that are foreign to the reality. To stop this you will have to fight off these disturbances and maintain focus on the moment at hand. This skill is called "Turning the mind."

Radical acceptance is not about deeming the situation as good or bad, allowing the prolongation of the situation or forsaking your options. It is about believing that everything is "as it is" and "as it should be". It is about accepting what is.

The individual is taught to focus on the present through the skills of mindfulness and distress tolerance.

Exercises for Distress Tolerance

Exercises for Accepting Reality

Observing Your Breath Exercise

Lie back on a bed, chair or whatever gives you comfort. Focus on your abdominal movement as you breathe gently and evenly. When you inhale, let your stomach rise to allow more air into the bottom half of your lungs. You will notice your stomach lower and your chest rise as air fills up the upper half of your lungs. Your inhaling will become shorter than your exhaling. Do this for ten breaths.

Half smile exercise for accepting reality

You can accept reality by using the body.

Without the support of a pillow or a mattress, lie back on a flat surface. Position your legs a little apart and lay your hands on the sides. Relax your muscles, neck, shoulder and face. Put on a half-smile—not a grin but a half-smile. Breathe gently and evenly. Let go of every muscle in your body. Lose yourself entirely as though you were a piece of silk floating in the air. Focus on your breathing. Continue this exercise for fifteen breathes.

Half-smile Exercise for Brief Moments

Take a minute of your free time to carry out this practice. Choose a spot, any spot. You can either stand or sit down for this. Focus one object; it could be a picture on the wall or a plant on the patio—just select something that is relatively still. Smile at it. Then quietly and gently inhale and exhale three times.

Half-smile to come to Peace with a Recent Conflict or Argument

Give a half-smile. Sit quietly and recall a conflict that took place recently, one that you felt strong emotions of anger and resentment for. Remember the event with as much detail as possible, enough to induce the anger you felt at the time it occurred. Remember all the bodily reactions you felt at the moment.

Now inhale three times and renew your half-smile. Put yourself in the position of the other person. You don't have to agree with them, but try to understand their view point. See what valid points he/she had in the argument. Remember the good qualities of the person, moments they have been kind to you. Let your compassion for the person diminish the resentment and anger you have within. Use the same situation to practice this exercise over and over again.

Worksheet of Distress Tolerance Pro's and Con's

	Pro's	Con's
Cope		
Not copping		

Final Words

Dialectical Behavior Therapy provides an ample of benefits as discussed earlier. The four modules (mindfulness, interpersonal effectiveness, emotional regulation, and distress tolerance) are designed to assist people with depression, anxiety, borderline personality disorder, eating disorder and much more.

Each module is interrelated to one another, and learning each component is essential to reaping the benefits of DBT.

It is the innate desire of this eBook that you acquire a greater understanding of DBT and its functions.

Remember: Life is not handed to us on a silver platter; everyone in this world is struggling with a specific issue—you're not alone.

Thank you for dedicating your time to read this eBook.

THE PROPERTY OF
DENISE COFFEE

Made in the USA
Columbia, SC
19 April 2018